Pieces of Gold

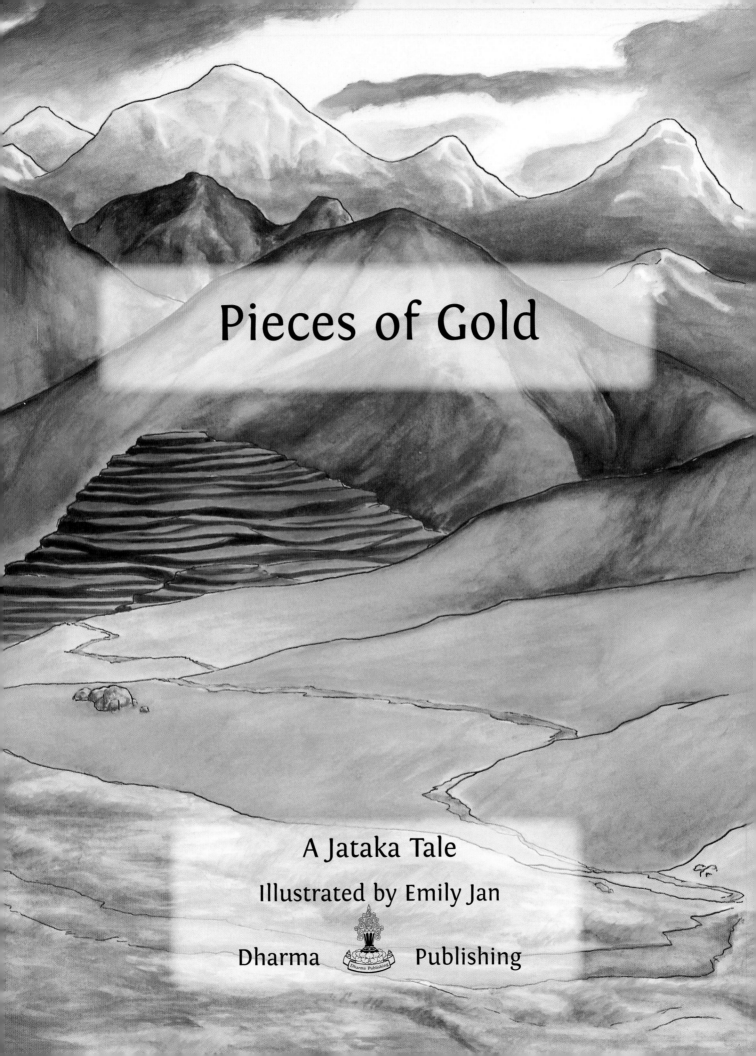

Pieces of Gold

A Jataka Tale

Illustrated by Emily Jan

Dharma Publishing

First published 2001

Second edition 2009, augmented with guidance for parents and teachers

Printed on acid-free paper

Printed in the United States of America by Dharma Press
35788 Hauser Bridge Road, Cazadero, California 95421

9   8   7   6   5   4   3   2

Library of Congress Cataloging-in-Publication Data

Pieces of Gold : A Jataka tale ; illustrated by Emily Jan

(Jataka Tales Series)
Summary: A young man tries to cheat his older brother, but in the end he realizes that his selfishness and dishonesty did not bring him happiness.

1.Jataka stories, English. [1. Jataka stories]
I. Jan, Emily, ill. II. Series
BQ1462.E5 P54 2001   294.3'82325—dc21   00-060136

ISBN 978-0-89800-432-8

Dedicated to children everywhere

Once upon a time in the far-off land of India a son was born to the family of a wealthy landowner. When the boy was still small, he was already known for his great kindness, and he grew up into a wealthy and wise young man. After his father died, he and his younger brother traveled to a village to collect a gift their father had left them. The two brothers received a thousand gold coins in a sack.

On the way home, the two brothers came to the river Ganges. While waiting on the shore for a boat to cross the river, they ate a simple meal. The elder brother threw his last bites of food into the water to feed the hungry fish. The Great River Spirit saw this and was pleased with this gift of food. Then the elder brother put his shirt on the sand, lay down upon it, closed his eyes and took a nap.

The younger brother, who was greedy by nature, wanted the gold for himself. He devised a way to steal it from his brother. He packed a sack of gravel to make it look like the sack of gold, and when they boarded the riverboat he snuck it onto the boat. When they approached the middle of the river where the water was deep, the younger brother pretended to stumble over something, and managed to drop the sack overboard.

"O brother, the gold has fallen into the water!" he cried. "What should we do now?" "There is nothing we can do," said the older brother gently. "We cannot get it back. What is gone is gone. It is best not to worry about it."

The Great River Spirit saw all that happened. She knew that the younger brother had mistakenly dropped the sack of gold into the river. Remembering the older brother's kindness towards the fish, she resolved to look out for him. She used her magical powers to look for a big-mouthed fish, and when she found one, she made him swallow the sack of gold.

When the greedy youth returned home, he hastily untied the sack he had kept under his vest, laughing in his sleeve about the trick he had played on his brother. But when he saw not the gold but the gravel spread out over the floor, he realized what he had done. In anguish, he fell onto his bed, clutching the bedpost.

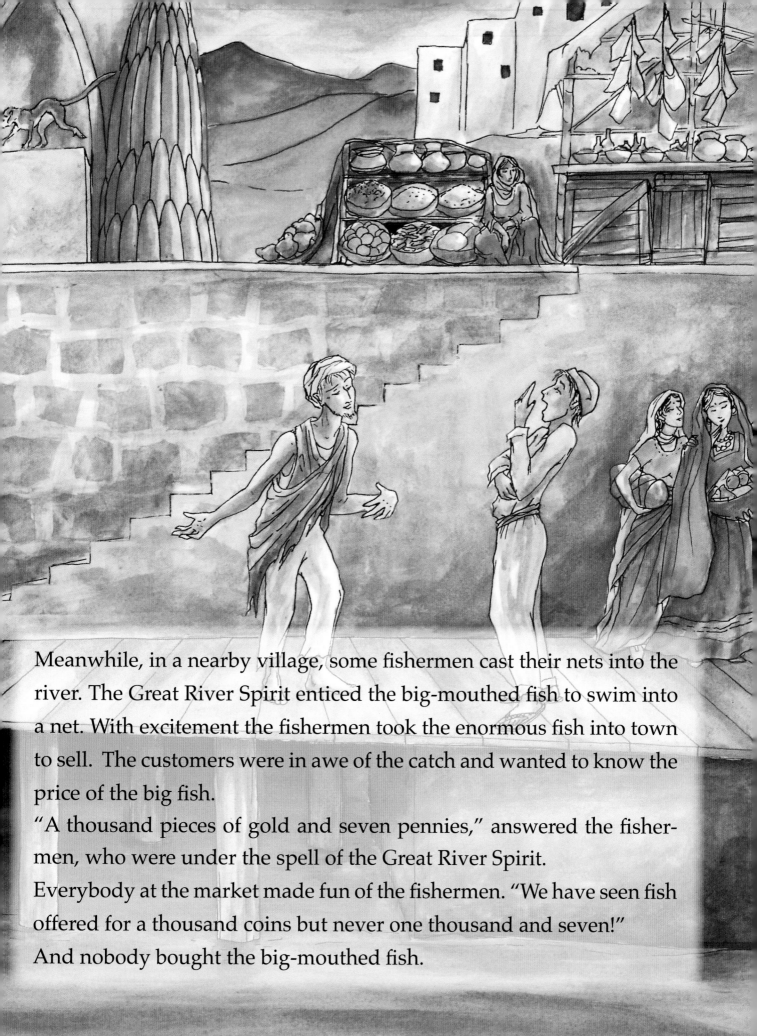

Meanwhile, in a nearby village, some fishermen cast their nets into the river. The Great River Spirit enticed the big-mouthed fish to swim into a net. With excitement the fishermen took the enormous fish into town to sell. The customers were in awe of the catch and wanted to know the price of the big fish.

"A thousand pieces of gold and seven pennies," answered the fishermen, who were under the spell of the Great River Spirit.

Everybody at the market made fun of the fishermen. "We have seen fish offered for a thousand coins but never one thousand and seven!"

And nobody bought the big-mouthed fish.

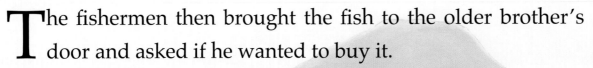

The fishermen then brought the fish to the older brother's door and asked if he wanted to buy it.

What is the price?" asked the older brother.

"You may have it for seven pennies," they answered, still under the spell of the Great River Spirit.

"How much did you ask other people to pay?"

"We asked others a thousand pieces of gold and seven pennies, but you can have it for just seven pennies," they answered.

What good luck!" he exclaimed. He paid the
seven pennies and gave the fish to his wife
to prepare a delicious meal. He said to her:
"Who would believe the story if it were told,
that this fish was to be sold
for a thousand pieces of gold?
It cost me only seven cents! How I wish
that everyone could buy this kind of fish!"

When his wife cut open the big-mouthed fish, imagine her surprise to find the sack of shiny gold!

She called her husband to come and see the great marvel. When he recognized the markings on the sack, he knew that the money belonged to him.

Amazed, the older brother wondered how it had come to pass that he had recovered the gold this way. Just then the River Spirit appeared in the air, whispering softly, "I am the Spirit of the River Ganges. You offered some of your food to the fish and I received the benefit from your kindness."

Then she recited the following verse:

"You fed the fish and made a gift to me.

I will always remember your generosity."

The Great River Spirit revealed to the older brother how his young brother had deceived him. "I have returned the coins to you, and warn you not to lose them again. Keep them for yourself! You must not give a single coin to your younger brother." Then she recited:

> *"There is no good fortune for the wicked heart,*
> *And in my blessing the wicked one has no part.*
> *He who cheats his brother out of their father's wealth,*
> *Works evil deeds by craft and stealth."*

With this, the Great River Spirit returned home to the Ganges.

It is true that I was wronged," said the older brother to his wife. "But this gold came to me through my father's generosity and it is only right that I share it with my brother." His wife, admiring his goodness, agreed that he should send his brother half of the thousand pieces of gold.

When the younger brother received the gold coins, he was filled with shame. He realized that his selfish and dishonest action had brought him no happiness, only suffering and pain. He resolved to change his ways, work hard and practice generosity from that day on.

My page

Colored by _____

PARENTS AND TEACHERS CORNER

The Jataka Tales nurture in readers young and old an appreciation for values shared by all the world's great spiritual traditions. Read aloud, performed and studied for centuries, they communicate universal values such kindness, forgiveness, compassion, humility, courage, honesty and patience. You can bring this story alive through the suggestions on these pages. Actively engaging with the stories creates a bridge to the children in your life and opens a dialogue about what brings joy, stability and caring.

Pieces of Gold

Two brothers travel to a village in the countryside of India to take care of their deceased father's estate. When they receive one thousand pieces of gold as inheritance, the younger brother is filled with greed. He tries to steal the gold, but in the process he loses it. The River Spirit magically returns the gold to the older brother who, in spite of every-thing, decides to share it with his younger bother. This generosity and kindness transforms the younger man's heart when he understands that his actions did not produce positive results, but only lead to pain.

Key Values
Forgiveness
Generosity
Goodness

Bringing the story to life

Engage the children by asking at the turning of the page: "What do you think will happen next?"

Asking children questions about the events and values in the story will deepen their understanding and enrich their vocabulary. For example:

• What does the elder brother do with his leftover bread?
• What mistake takes place on the boat?
• How is a fish involved in returning the gold?
• Why does the older brother decide to share the money with his younger sibling, who deceived him?
• Do you know how it feels to want something that belongs to someone else and secretly try to get it?

Discussion topics and questions can be modified depending on the child's age.

Learning through play

Children love to try out new ideas and use all five senses to make discoveries. Use the story to encourage their creativity and help them explore the characters:

- Have the children color in or draw a scene or character that intrigues them. Then invite them to talk about what it means to them, exploring the key values.
- Make masks for each character.
- Paint the masks and decorate them.
- Let each child choose a character to impersonate. Imitate the voices and and bring the qualities of the two brothers, the Great River Spirit, the big-mouthed fish and the fishermen to life. Then switch roles.
- Have the children re-tell you the story, and explain why the characters act the way they do.

Active reading

- Even before children can read, they enjoy storybooks and love growing familiar with the characters and drawings. You can show them the pictures in this book and tell the story in your own words.
- Some Jatakas include unusual words, so you can prepare by reading the book first yourself. By reading the book to the children a few times and helping them recognize words, they begin to build vocabulary.
- Children love to hear the same story over and over, with different and sometimes exaggerated voices for each character.
- Intgrate the wisdom of the story into everyday life. When tempers flare or patience is called for, remind the child of the older brother's generosity.
- Talk about the story while you and the child are engaged in daily activities like washing the dishes or driving to school.
- Display the key values and refer to them in your daily interactions.

Names and places

India: The source of many spiritual traditions and the background of most of the Jatakas (accounts of the Buddha's previous lives). People seeking wisdom have always viewed India's forests and jungles as favorable places for solitary retreats. The Buddha taught the Jatakas to clarify the workings of karma, the relationship between actions and results.

River Ganges: Winding 1,500 miles across northern India, this great river is revered as a goddess and plays a role in numerous myths.

The Great River Spirit: Also known as the Goddess of the Ganges. According to most spiritual traditions, nature spirits exist in a world parallel to our own, and their task is to protect the environment. They can be quite powerful. In myths they are portrayed as personal beings.

The Jataka Tales are folk tales that were transmitted orally, memorized and passed from generation to generation for hundreds of years. We are grateful for the opportunity to offer them to you. May they inspire fresh insight into the dynamics of human relationships and may understanding grow with each reading.

The Jataka Tales are for children aged three to eight

JATAKA TALES SERIES